believe

WRITTEN & COMPILED BY DAN ZADRA & KOBI YAMADA

DESIGNED BY JESSICA PHOENIX & VANESSA TIPPMANN

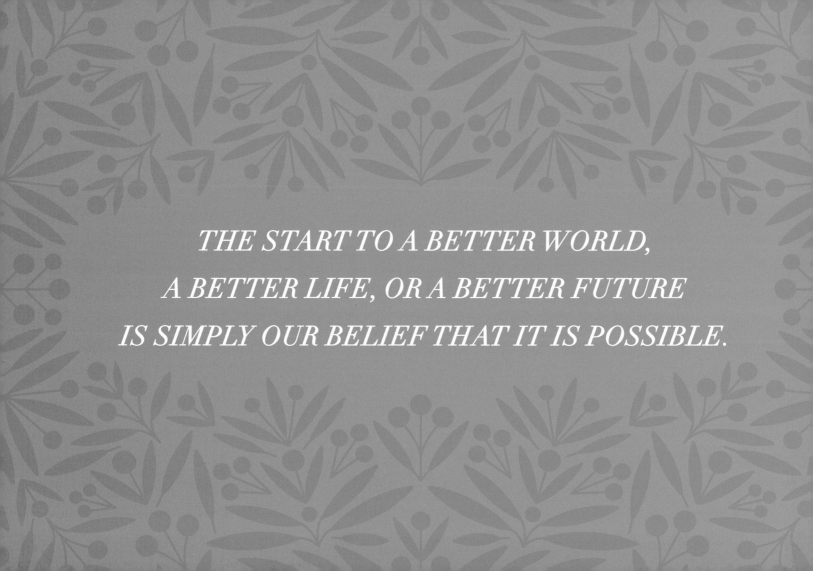

THE START TO A BETTER WORLD,
A BETTER LIFE, OR A BETTER FUTURE
IS SIMPLY OUR BELIEF THAT IT IS POSSIBLE.

There's a lot in this world we can't see. But just because we can't see something, or hold it in our hands, doesn't mean it isn't there. This is especially true in difficult times, on those days when all you can see with your eyes are the problems. But if you look with your heart, you will see that possibility is all around you—and in you.

Because some things have to be believed before they can be seen. Because your hopes, dreams, and aspirations really are achievable. And because there is so much courage, goodness, and potential in you—that once you begin to believe, the world you want becomes possible.

BELIEVE IN FRESH STARTS AND NEW BEGINNINGS.

The capacity for hope is the most significant fact of life. It provides human beings with a sense of destination and the energy to get started.

NORMAN COUSINS

BELIEVE THAT OPPORTUNITY IS EVERYWHERE AND ALL AROUND YOU.

People will try to tell you that all the great opportunities have been snapped up. In reality, the world changes every second, blowing new opportunities in all directions, including yours.

KEN HAKUTA

BELIEVE THAT THE UNIVERSE IS FRIENDLY AND LIFE IS ON YOUR SIDE.

What is life for? It is for you.

ABRAHAM MASLOW

BELIEVE YOU ARE A
ONCE-IN-ALL-HISTORY EVENT.

Be faithful to that which exists
nowhere but in yourself...

ANDRÉ GIDE

BELIEVE YOU ARE HERE
FOR A REASON.

Believe in something big.
Your life is worth a noble motive.

WALTER ANDERSON

BELIEVE THAT NOTHING IS TOO GOOD TO BE TRUE.

Life is the most wonderful fairy tale...

HANS CHRISTIAN ANDERSEN

BELIEVE YOU MUST
TAKE YOUR CHANCE.

Act boldly and unseen forces will come to your aid.

DOROTHEA BRANDE

BELIEVE WHEN OTHERS MIGHT NOT.

To be nobody-but-yourself—in a world which is doing its best, night and day, to make you everybody else— means to fight the hardest battle which any human being can fight; and never stop fighting.

E E CUMMINGS

BELIEVE THAT PASSION PERSUADES.

...everything in life responds to the song of the heart.

ERNEST HOLMES

BELIEVE IN DOING GREAT WORK.

The key is to trust your heart to move where your unique talents can flourish. This old world will really spin when work becomes a joyous expression of the soul.

AL SACHAROV

BELIEVE THERE IS ALWAYS, ALWAYS, ALWAYS A WAY.

When you have exhausted all possibilities,
remember this: you haven't.

THOMAS EDISON

BELIEVE YOU ARE FAR BIGGER THAN ANYTHING THAT CAN HAPPEN TO YOU.

In your life's journey, there will be excitement and fulfillment, boredom and routine… But when you have picked a dream that is bigger than you personally, that truly reflects the ideals that you cherish, and that can positively affect others, then you will always have another reason for carrying on.

PAMELA MELROY

BELIEVE THERE'S A LIGHT AT THE END OF THE TUNNEL.

Hope begins in the dark, the stubborn
hope that if you just show up and try to do
the right thing, the dawn will come.
You wait and watch and work:
you don't give up.

ANNE LAMOTT

BELIEVE YOU MIGHT BE THAT LIGHT FOR SOMEONE ELSE.

You do build in darkness if you have faith.
When the light returns you have made of yourself
a fortress… you may even find yourself needed
and sought by others as a beacon in their dark.

OLGA ROSMANITH

BELIEVE THAT
LIFE IS SACRED.

Listen to your life. See it for the fathomless mystery that it is. ...touch, taste, smell your way to the holy and hidden heart of it because in the last analysis all moments are key moments, and life itself is grace.

FREDERICK BUECHNER

BELIEVE THAT
THE LITTLE THINGS
AREN'T LITTLE.

We can only be said to be alive
in those moments when our hearts
are conscious of our treasures.

THORNTON WILDER

BELIEVE YOU ARE BLESSED.

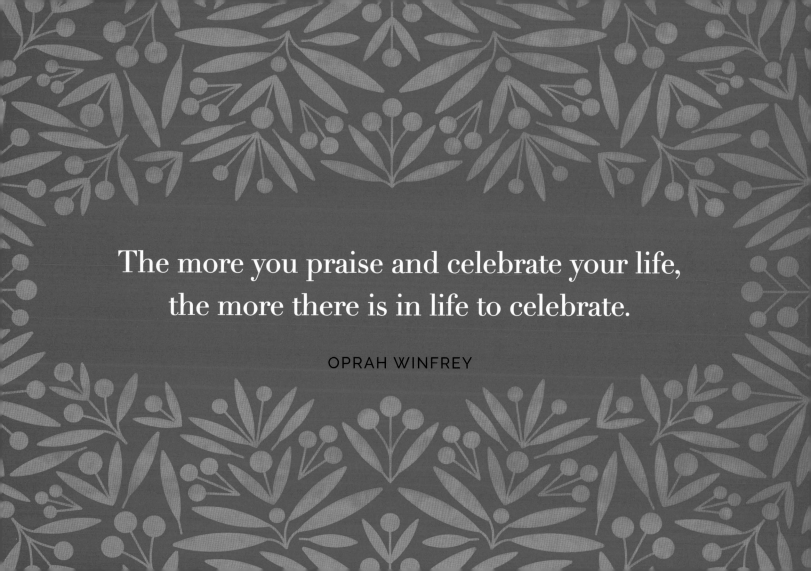

The more you praise and celebrate your life,
the more there is in life to celebrate.

OPRAH WINFREY

BELIEVE IN THE MIRACLE
OF THE SECOND CHANCE.

The life you have led doesn't need
to be the only life you have.

ANNA QUINDLEN

BELIEVE IN GIVING BACK.

To enjoy the journey is to leap into people's lives. To enjoy the journey is to give until the stretch is a sacrifice. The question always is: what is it in life that will pull you out of your seat to be brave, risk and serve?

JANIE JASIN

BELIEVE IN LOVE AND EVERYTHING IT TOUCHES.

…we all have the power to give away love, to love other people. And if we do so, we change the kind of person we are, and we change the kind of world we live in.

HAROLD KUSHNER

BELIEVE THE BEST ABOUT OTHERS.

You can work miracles by having faith in others.
By choosing to think and believe the best about
people, you are able to bring out the best in them.

BOB MOAWAD

BELIEVE THAT FRIENDSHIP IS AN HONOR AND PRIVILEGE.

If you want trust, trust others. If you want respect, respect others. If you want help, help others. If you want love and peace in your life, give them away. If you want great friends, be one. That's how it works.

DAN ZADRA

BELIEVE IN TAKING A STAND.

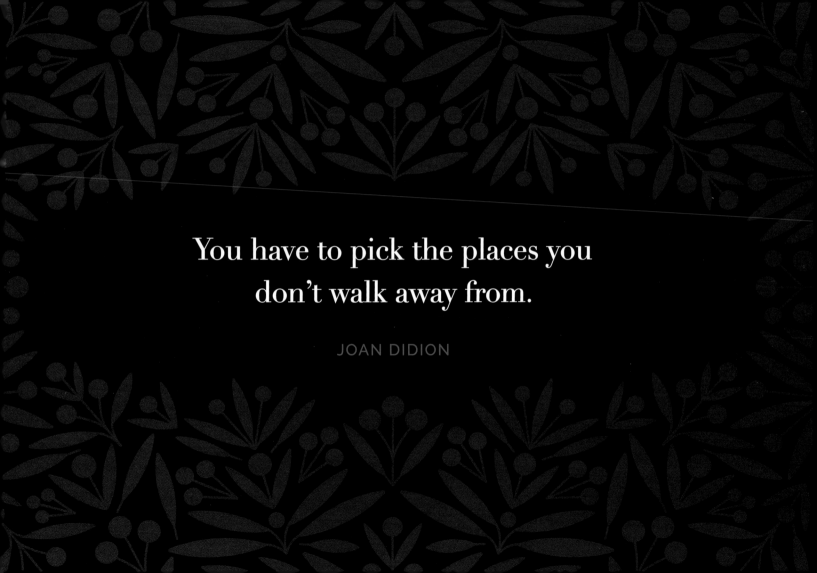

You have to pick the places you
don't walk away from.

JOAN DIDION

BELIEVE IN DOING THE RIGHT THING BECAUSE IT'S RIGHT.

Look the world straight in the eye.

HELEN KELLER

BELIEVE YOU CAN MAKE A DIFFERENCE.

We won't always know whose lives we touched and made better for our having cared, because actions can sometimes have unforeseen ramifications. What's important is that you do care and you act.

CHARLOTTE LUNSFORD BERRY

BELIEVE THAT TOGETHER WE ARE BETTER.

What I do, you cannot do; but what you do, I cannot do. The needs are great, and none of us, including me, ever do great things. But we can all do small things, with great love, and together we can do something wonderful.

MOTHER TERESA

BELIEVE WE CAN BUILD A BETTER WORLD.

How lovely to think that no one need wait a moment. We can start now, start slowly, changing the world. How lovely that everyone, great and small, can make a contribution toward introducing justice straightaway. And you can always, always give something, even if it is only kindness!

ANNE FRANK

BELIEVE IN TODAY.

Life is a great and wondrous mystery, and the only thing we know that we have for sure is what is right here right now. Don't miss it.

LEO BUSCAGLIA

BELIEVE THAT THE
BEST IS YET TO BE.

You have powers you never dreamed of.
You can do things you never thought you could
do. There are no limitations in what you can do
except the limitation of your own mind.

DARWIN P. KINGSLEY

BELIEVE IN YOURSELF.

COMPENDIUM®

live inspired

WITH SPECIAL THANKS TO THE ENTIRE COMPENDIUM FAMILY.

CREDITS:

WRITTEN & COMPILED BY: DAN ZADRA & KOBI YAMADA
EDITED BY: KRISTIN EADE
DESIGNED BY: VANESSA TIPPMANN
ART DIRECTION BY: JESSICA PHOENIX

ISBN: 978-1-943200-35-1